# Protecting Parent-Child Bonds

## The 28th Amendment

**Authors:**
Ron B Palmer
Sherry L Palmer

Publisher

GULF STREAM PRESS

© 2013 - 2017 Ronald B Palmer and Sherry L Palmer, Printed and Bound in the United Sates of America. All rights reserved. No part of this book may be reproduced or transmitted in any form or by any means, electronic or mechanical, including photocopying, recording, or by an information storage and retrieval system—except by a reviewer who may quote brief passages in a review to be printed in a magazine, newspaper, or on the Web—without permission in writing from the copyright holders. For more information, please contact Publisher@GulfStreamPress.com.

Although the author and publisher have made every effort to ensure the accuracy and completeness of information contained in this book, we assume no responsibility for errors, inaccuracies, omissions, or any inconsistency herein. Any slights of people, places, or organizations are unintentional.

ISBN-13: 978-1494821517

ISBN-10: 1494821516

BOOK VERSION: 2017-P001

Due to changes in the publishing industry it is possible to update books on a more frequent schedule than was previously possible. In order to aide use of this book as a reference source the publisher has added a version number that will be incrimented with each update.

First Printing 2014

ATTENTION CORPORATIONS, UNIVERSITIES, COLLEGES, AND PROFESSIONAL ORGANIZATIONS: Quantity discounts are available on bulk purchases of this book for educational, gift purposes, or as premiums for increasing magazine subscriptions or renewals. Special books or book excerpts can also be created to accommodate specific needs. For information, please contact Gulf Stream Press, Publisher@GulfStreamPress.com.

## DEDICATION

This book is dedicated to the spirit of Thomas Paine and his profound work titled *"Common Sense"*, the introduction to Paine's incredibly impactful work is copied here:

> *Perhaps the sentiments contained in the following pages, are not yet sufficiently fashionable to procure them general favor; a long habit of not thinking a thing wrong, gives it a superficial appearance of being right, and raises at first a formidable outcry in defense of custom. But tumult soon subsides. Time makes more converts than reason.*
>
> *As a long and violent abuse of power is generally the means of calling the right of it in question, (and in matters too which might never have been thought of, had not the sufferers been aggravated into the inquiry,) and as the king of England hath undertaken in his own right, to support the parliament in what he calls theirs, and as the good people of this country are grievously oppressed by the combination, they have an undoubted privilege to inquire into the pretensions of both, and equally to reject the usurpations of either.*
>
> *In the following sheets, the author hath studiously avoided every thing which is personal among ourselves. Compliments as well as censure to individuals make no part thereof. The wise and the worthy need not the triumph of a pamphlet; and those whose sentiments are injudicious or unfriendly, will cease of themselves, unless too much pains is bestowed upon their conversion.*
>
> *The cause of America is, in a great measure, the cause of all mankind. Many circumstances have, and will arise, which are not local, but universal, and through which the principles of all lovers of mankind are affected, and in the event of which, their affections are interested. The laying a country desolate with fire and sword, declaring war against the natural rights of all mankind, and extirpating the defenders thereof from the face of the earth, is the concern of every man to whom nature hath given the power of feeling; of which class, regardless of party censure, is the AUTHOR.*

**—Philadelphia, Feb. 14, 1776, (Published Anonymously)**

## SPECIAL THANKS

We would like to offer special thanks to Tina Granstrom, President PAS Intervention — Florida Chapter and Catherine MacWillie, Retired Police Officer, President Custody Calculations, and divorce coach for their particular help during the editing and review process for this book.

# Table of Contents

**Chapter 1**
INTRODUCTION ..................................................... 1

**Chapter 2**
THE AMENDMENT ................................................. 7

**Chapter 3**
THE FAMILY UNIT CLAUSE ................................... 11

**Chapter 4**
THE FITNESS CLAUSE ........................................... 17

**Chapter 5**
THE RIGHTS OF FIT PARENTS .............................. 29

**Chapter 6**
THE NATURAL RIGHTS CLAUSE ........................... 43

**Chapter 7**
THE CARE CUSTODY CONTROL AND POSSESSION CLAUSE ................................................................. 49

**Chapter 8**
THE HEALTH SAFETY AND WELFARE CLAUSE ......... 55

**Chapter 9**
 THE AUTHORS' FINAL WORDS ............................. 59

# Chapter 1

## INTRODUCTION

Many of you will know us from our prior book "NOT In the Child's Best Interest." This book goes into great detail about the constitutional arguments in favor of parental rights and children's rights.

If you are in a custody battle right now you do not need an amendment to have parental rights. You have them already naturally. You should be doing everything you can to protect your rights as provided under the constitution right now. Some of you already know and may have heard us say that we don't need a constitutional amendment to have parental rights because you already have them naturally. We stand by that and our previous book helps you understand what those rights are, where they come from, and how to protect them.

What we are all faced with today is a comprehensive attack, through judicial abuse of power, on our parental rights and we need a comprehensive political response to that attack. This book provides a powerful tool for a political response that in many ways is based on the tactics used by the women's rights movement.

Between 1923 and 1972 the Equal Rights Amendment (ERA) became a lightning rod political tool. Woman's rights groups leveraged the proposed amendment to rally people to the cause of equal rights for women. Although the amendment was ultimately defeated, the political momentum it created served to get other laws passed and spurred Supreme Court rulings that ultimately acknowledged equal rights for women.

## Protecting Parent-Child Bonds

We believe that the ERA served as a focal point and a powerful tool in the women's rights struggle, and we are proposing this Amendment (the Parent-Child Bond Amendment) as our "rallying cry" with a strong focus on getting it passed, but also as a focal point for political debate. Like the ERA, this amendment is proposed so that people everywhere will have an easy way to let their politicians know that they are fed up and the time has come for states to stop violating and start fully respecting parent-child bonds.

The introduction of a constitutional amendment can be a powerful force for good and a catalyst for change. As an activist you can use this book to open up another front in the war for protecting parental and child rights. This book can serve to help you get more people on board with the basic idea that parents have rights with their children, that children are best protected when parental rights are protected, and that those rights must receive the highest level of constitutional protection.

This Amendment and book help you present these issues to your elected representatives in a coherent and meaningful way and allow more parents to become involved and effective without having to master the complex constitutional arguments. Parents can simply point this book out to their Representatives and tell them, I support this proposed amendment, why don't you. The book itself will convey the details of the argument.

As you may know, there is already a constitutional amendment proposal being circulated by another organization. While that proposed amendment would do much to help some parents, it leaves many other parents out in the cold, particularly parents in divorce or for any situation where parental rights are in conflict with another biological or legal parent. We believe that this proposed amendment is much more comprehensive and will do much more to protect parents and children alike.

Having spent thousands of hours reading countless Supreme Court and lesser court opinions, we have become expert in the ways that courts justify defying the Constitution and failing to protect parental rights. We are certain that even under the other

## Chapter 1 — INTRODUCTION

proposed Amendment that the courts would continue denying parental rights just as they are doing today. Nothing, in that amendment's language overcomes current flawed thinking by the courts. Our proposed amendment, on the other hand, has real teeth that courts cannot easily ignore or easily twist to suit their personal prejudices and biases. It is specifically crafted to equally protect all parents, married, single, and divorced, as well as children.

We have also become very familiar with the ways higher Courts leave openings in their opinions to except protection for children of divorce. These openings allow lower courts to treat divorcing parents as second-class citizens and to continue the rein of destruction to parent-child bonds in divorce. We have taken the time to specifically craft a proposed constitutional amendment that we believe addresses the majority of flawed reasoning used by courts today and that will provide strong protection of parents and children in most circumstances. Our hope is that this book will generate real discussion and real action on crafting and passing a constitutional amendment and improving family codes that strongly protect healthy parent-child bonds for all parents, married, single, and divorced.

While we have worked hard on crafting the language of this amendment, we know that any amendment that finally gets approved will have input from many points of view. For this reason, we have laid out our reasoning in this book for why we included each idea and concept in this amendment and have made our case for this reasoning so that these ideas can be preserved. We have also included an in-depth analysis of why each sentence was included and why almost every word is essential to the protection of our liberties.

With a groundswell of support, this amendment could be passed in a few years' time. Meanwhile, we continue to encourage you as parents to remain focused on any immediate court battle you may be going through. You can win through the courts by changing the way the custody game is played, by asserting your constitutional rights. Where divorce court judges continue abusing their power we win as a whole by challenging abuse after abuse in appeal after appeal until we have built up a body of case law

## Protecting Parent-Child Bonds

sufficient to provide the protections parents and children deserve. This was how women gained equal rights even as they fought a very public battle around the ERA.

> NOTE FOR PARENTS: If you are facing denial of your rights today, you have reason for hope and support for action in many of the Court's current rulings. Do NOT wait on this amendment to pass. Fight for your rights today. Use the reasoning and case citations you will find in our other book, *"NOT In the Child's Best Interest"*, to get the best results in your case today. Meanwhile, you can increase the pressure on your local courts by sharing this amendment with every legislator and politician in your county and State. The very act of many parents fighting for the protection of their rights at the trial court level as well as politically will move more and more divorce court judges towards equal parenting.

The women's rights movement went through many years of fighting to pass the Equal Rights Amendment. That Amendment would have protected women's rights equally with men's. Ultimately, an abundance of Supreme Court rulings in this area produced an environment of equal protection for women even though the Amendment did not get fully ratified.

### Was this a loss or a win for women?

The women's movement pursued a two-front campaign and they reached their goal. We believe it was a major win regardless of which front in the campaign was successful. Each front gained strength from the other and the campaign succeeded. We are proposing the same be done for parental rights and are officially opening up our second front in this movement with the release of this book.

We are not the first to propose an Amendment but we believe that we are the first to share so much of our reasoning in a format that you can so easily use to promote the vision of equal rights for

## Chapter 1 — INTRODUCTION

all parents and protected parent-child bonds.

**Please, recommend this book to anyone who will listen.**

# Chapter 2

## THE AMENDMENT

Constitutional language is by necessity very different from the language used in statutes. A constitution both organizes a government and provides a core set of principles for which that government is created to protect.

Principles are stated in a language that is simultaneously specific and vague. For example, the terms "liberty" and "equal protection" that are found in the Fourteenth Amendment are precise terms in that boundaries can be drawn around their meaning sufficiently to create more specific laws. At the same time, these terms are also vague.

Much of the freedom we experience today has evolved from the efforts of the Courts to establish the precise boundaries that confine the meaning of these terms. Nowhere in the Constitution are the "right to vote" or the "right to travel freely within and between states" to be found. They are, however, firmly established fundamental rights precisely because the Supreme Court has found them to be within the boundaries of the word liberty as used in the Fourteenth Amendment. In addition, they have been identified as liberties that are fundamental and necessary to our very way of life and the preservation of the wider "ordered liberty" we all enjoy.

Rights that are listed in the form of Amendments to the Constitution are by their nature "fundamental" rights, but they are not the only fundamental rights. The United States Supreme Court has said that parents have a fundamental right to the care, custody, and control of their children and yet state courts deprive us of these rights daily. When we state these rights as we have done here in an actual Amendment, they take on a degree of acceptance that is unsurpassed in our system of laws. By stating these rights in an Amendment, we make it much easier for state courts to understand their boundaries and harder for state courts to ignore these rights and much harder for them to deprive people of these rights.

Our objective, in crafting the language of this amendment, is to firmly establish principles regarding the rights of parents and minor children that end the current state of abuse and tyranny; rights that can grow over time; and rights that can be appropriately limited in scope. The Amendment does not cover every conceivable detail that Courts might face, but it states the core principles forcefully enough that Courts will have considerable guidance in what "we the people" say is acceptable and what is not.

Immediately following this chapter is our proposed text for the 28th Amendment to the U.S. Constitution. The chapters that follow will describe the reason behind each clause of the proposed amendment and the reasoning behind choosing certain words for the Amendment. We want you to be able to see how every word fits together forming a shield of protection for you and your child.

We sincerely hope that this book provokes a vigorous debate in our society, in the legal community, and among our political leaders that results in the protection for parents and for children of their most cherished parent-child bonds. The result we are looking for are bonds that are strongly protected from State invasion except upon clear proof of harm to a child in the form of clear and present danger using the highest level of due process protection.

On the next page you will find the full text of the proposed Amendment. Following this chapter, each clause will be addressed individually in its own chapter. The authors will explain why each clause is important and why each clause is worded the way it is. These chapters are intended to bring out the principles that we feel must be addressed in a constitutional amendment for that amendment to truly protect parent-child bonds.

## Chapter 2 — THE AMENDMENT
## The Text of the Amendment

*1.  The most basic form of a protected private family unit is an individual parent and their minor child. The state may neither sever nor cross the boundaries of this family unit, except upon unfitness of the parent. Parent and child share a right to free and equal association with each other.*

*2.  A parent is assumed to be fit until the state proves that either (a) the parent has exposed the minor child to clear and present danger as a result of the parent's decisions (b) the parent is incapable of meeting the minimum basic needs of the child for a significantly prolonged period (c) the parent is unwilling to meet the minimum basic needs of the minor child (d) a parent knowingly and intelligently waives their parental rights.*

*(1)  Fit parents are entrusted by nature or the State with determining the best interests of their minor child and must be assumed to be acting in their child's best interests unless proven unfit*

*(2)  Each fit parent has the equal right and duty to direct and control their minor child's education, to include educating the minor child through personal example, which arises through routine parenting of the child. The child has a right to receive education from each parent equally. These rights are among the penumbra of individual First Amendment rights.*

*(3)  Fit parents hold equal rights and duties in the care, custody, control, and physical possession of the minor child. Any conflict between these rights must be resolved in as equal a manner as possible.*

*(4)  Fit parents may entrust certain of these rights to others as they see fit without forfeiting their rights.*

*3.  The rights of natural (biological) parents are neither established nor granted by the State but are self-evident rights that shall be protected by the State and by this Amendment. The State may create legal parents where that creation does not unduly burden the rights of natural parents without their consent to the burden. Once established, except where specifically limited, legal parents are granted protection under this Amendment.*

*4. Minor children have the right to be in the care, custody, control, and possession of their fit parents equally, and where no fit parents exist, to be in the care, custody, control, and possession of the State. All other rights with which the minor child is endowed but is incapable of exercising are to be held in trust by fit parents in the first instance and by the State only where no fit parent exists.*

*5. Nothing in this Amendment shall be construed as limiting the State from setting minimum, equally applicable, standards or regulation concerning the general health, safety, and welfare of its citizens. When rights between parents are in conflict and the State is asked to intervene, that intervention shall be the least detrimental to these rights. Where a valid question of harm to the child exists, the State may act to protect the child for the briefest time necessary to protect the child from that immediate harm.*

# Chapter 3

## THE FAMILY UNIT CLAUSE

***1. The most basic form of a protected private family unit is an individual parent and their minor child. The state may neither sever nor cross the boundaries of this family unit, except upon unfitness of the parent. Parent and child share a right to free and equal association with each other.***

Prior to our Constitution and certainly prior to the Fourteenth Amendment, many States tied parental rights and inheritance rights to legally recognized marriages. These ideas were codified in the "Bastardy Laws" which have long since been overturned by the U.S. Supreme Court and have disappeared from our state law codes. When these laws were in effect, any child of the marriage became the husband's child. Any child that the husband fathered outside of the marriage was considered a bastard, a second-class citizen in many respects, and the father was allowed few if any rights to that child. Often, even the mother wasn't allowed rights to the child. Many times the child became the ward of or property of the town, city, or state.

During these times children were considered a peculiar form of property. Typically, the father was endowed with "rights" over the child which included rights to the wages of the child. This was common even after the Fourteenth Amendment was ratified as this quote from a Georgia Supreme Court opinion makes clear, "Hence in any provision made by the law for the taking out of the custody of the parent a minor child, unless the parent is given a reasonable opportunity to be heard on the question as to whether the conditions are such that the State should deprive him, either temporarily or until the child becomes of full age, of his custody and services and labor, the parent would be under the operation of such proceeding deprived of his property without due process of law." Kennedy v. Meara, (1906), Supreme Court of Georgia.

In many ways, parents, fathers at least, had better protected rights when children were considered property than either parent has today.

Later years found the rights of parents described in terms of the fundamental liberties introduced in the Due Process clause of the Fourteenth Amendment. The state courts however did not integrate these into their practices and instead the path that parental rights has taken is as follows: For a time, rights remained with the father and then gradually over time as the woman's movement gained power, the rights shifted primarily to the mother, as we saw in the "tender years doctrine". Following rulings of the U.S. Supreme Court that stated discrimination couldn't be based on sex, these rights became recognized as belonging to either both parents equally or as a remnant of the Bastardy Laws as being a part of the marital rights. Still parental rights are not integrated properly into family court practices.

Further rulings by the Supreme Court have made clear that rights must be the same for married and single alike and that parental rights attach (are tied) to individuals. These Supreme Court opinions have forever destroyed any legal claim that parental rights are tied to a marriage. No matter how much the concept of parental rights being dependent on marriage has been shown to be unconstitutional; many people, judges and legislators included; still have a deep-seated emotional bias favoring marriage and penalizing divorce. This, we believe, is a major source of the bias and prejudice that destroys parent-child bonds in divorce courts every day.

With this history as context, we offer the Family Unit Clause as a definitive statement regarding the relationship that is protected and the nature of that protection. These rights are individual rights and they are held by each individual parent and each

## Chapter 3 — THE FAMILY UNIT CLAUSE

individual child. These rights are inalienable, meaning that even where they may be rightfully or wrongfully denied, their relationship to the individual can never be severed. The parent-child relationship that these rights protect, between a parent and a child, is the very basis of family integrity and the family's right to privacy.

The state may extend privacy protections to the marital bond as well, but it may NOT sever the parent-child bond based on marital status or a change in marital status. This right to privacy comes irrespective of the marital status of the parent or whether other parents may be living. This right to privacy comes irrespective of how many children there may be and it exists between each parent and each child uniquely. Privacy rights have been granted the highest level of scrutiny by the Supreme Court and this right is phrased here as a privacy right to set the expectation that it continue to enjoy that highest level of protection.

This clause goes on to make clear that this relationship is protected from invasion by the State except for some very narrow conditions that are listed in the Fitness Clause. Specifically, the parties to this relationship have the right to be left alone by the Government. This means that the Government may NOT reach into the relationship and override any of the decisions made within the relationship except where that intervention is couched in broadly and equally applicable laws that are designed to protect the health, safety, and welfare of people generally.

Divorce is NOT one of these decisions that allow the state to reach into the relationship or override any of the decisions made within the relationship, or to force continuation of any of the decisions made within a marital relationship, or to force continuation of any of the decisions made within a marital relationship, not even at the request of the other parent.

A significant function and duty of parents in raising children is to determine how much risk a child is exposed to as part of growing up and learning life lessons. Children protected from all risk fail to grow and they become incapable adults.

Reasonable people can have wildly different opinions regard-

## Protecting Parent-Child Bonds

ing appropriate levels of risk for a child, but nobody can credibly argue that children must be or even can be protected from all risk. The State should intervene in decisions regarding relative risk in only the broadest and most widely applicable circumstances or in specific circumstances where the risk goes well beyond the very wide range of "normal" or "generally acceptable."

Immunizations are an issue that has broad applicability. Parents <u>must</u> make a personal determination regarding the risk associated with immunizing a child as opposed to the risk of not immunizing a child. While that is essentially a personal protected choice, the failure of large numbers of people to immunize their children can cause epidemics of the disease even in people who have significant protection from the immunization.

In this area, the government has a valid role in taking measures to ensure that the critical mass of people immunize their children. This exposes a situation where the rights of the individual parent to take risks for their own child conflicts with the right of the people at large to protect themselves from threats of epidemic through government action. In these kinds of situations, it is expected that the parent's right to choose for their child is almost but not quite as strong as their right to choose for themselves.

The previous statement will get many parent's attention. What exactly do we mean by limiting the totality of the parent's right?

There is an unfortunately common scenario where, mostly for religious reasons, people may refuse medical treatment. To this point courts have generally held that adults can make the choice to refuse medical treatment and their privacy rights prevent the government from forcing them to receive medical treatment. That choice is perfectly fine for that adult to make. They pay the price of that choice directly and governmental choice restriction, regardless of outcome, would be a severe blow to personal freedom principles.

When it comes to the child's rights that are held in trust by a fit parent, the parent does NOT pay the price for that choice direct-

## Chapter 3 — THE FAMILY UNIT CLAUSE

ly and the choice is potentially fatal and irreversible for the child. In these extreme situations, it is certainly appropriate for the State to step in and ascertain the true motives for that choice, for while it must be presumed that parents act in their child's best interests generally, in situations of extreme potential harm to the child, it is reasonable and appropriate for the State to require more than a presumption of acting in the child's best interests.

This issue is NOT one of recognizing a State power or of granting a State power. It is an issue of preserving the rights of the child to make their own decisions when they reach the age of majority. If a parent takes on risks for a child that are out of all proportion to the wide range of reasonable and acceptable risk in a child's life, it is reasonable for society as a whole, through its government, to act in a manner consistent with preserving the individual child's right to choose for themselves, at a later date. For only if they reach maturity will they have the opportunity to choose for themselves. In these extreme circumstances, it is expected that this Amendment both gives great respect to the parent's rights but also ensures that the child will have a reasonable chance to live to exercise their own rights themselves.

It is recognized that the State has *parens patriae* interest in all of its citizens, meaning that the State is the ultimate caretaker when other more appropriate caretakers are unavailable. This Amendment attempts to make clear that the State's interest is subordinate to and secondary to the parent's and the child's rights. *Parens patriae* authority, however, may only be invoked in very specific circumstances where there is clear and convincing evidence that the parent is NOT acting in the child's best interests and only when the highest level of protection for procedural and substantive due process are used. Very specific triggers must be reached before the State's parens patriae interests are allowed to trump the parent's rights.

It should be clear that before the State may intervene it must meet a three-prong, strict scrutiny test. It must prove a compelling state interest sufficient to overcome a fundamental right. It must provide a law that is narrowly tailored to achieve only that interest. And, it must prove that the resultant State action is the action

## Protecting Parent-Child Bonds

that least restricts the right in question.

This test must be applied in matters of procedural due process, substantive due process, and equal protection. In other words the State cannot treat fit divorcing parents differently than fit married parents or fit single parents without proving a compelling interest to do so and meeting the other two prongs of the test. Vague claims of harm to a child because of divorce is simply insufficient grounds for the State to intervene in child custody issues.

This clause also mentions that a parent and a child create a family unit. This goes against the old premise that a family unit was only the nuclear family unit and after divorce only one parent could continue as the child's family unit. The Supreme Court has now made clear that parental rights are individual in nature and do not depend on marriage. This statement in this amendment stamps out completely any lingering State enforced bias against divorce in the parental rights debate.

Divorce courts are continuing in the unconstitutional momentum that held parental rights to be a function of marriage. They still act as if only one parent has rights, that the other parent is only a visitor, that the other parent only has duties to the child not rights, and that the other parent is a nuisance to the parent with rights. The current momentum creates two fundamentally unequal parents; one first-class parent and one second-class parent. The current momentum assumes that parents in divorce are NOT deserving of equal treatment under the law.

This clause serves to make clear that NO State may treat single, divorced, or divorcing parents as second-class citizens or as having lesser parental rights than married parents. This clause makes clear that the protected private right is between "individual" parents and "individual" children. By nature children are part of two distinct family units, one with the mother and one with the father. While marriage may confer additional rights upon the married couple, the lack of a marital union may NOT be used to deny rights so fundamental as the right to maintain a parent-child bond.

# Chapter 4

## THE FITNESS CLAUSE

*2. A parent is assumed to be fit until the state proves that either a) the parent has exposed the minor child to clear and present danger as a result of the parent's decisions b) the parent is incapable of meeting the minimum reasonable needs of the child for a significantly prolonged period c) the parent is unwilling to meet the minimum reasonable needs of the minor child d) a parent knowingly and intelligently waives their parental rights.*

    States have a very bad track record with parental rights. They remove, limit, deprive, and deny parental rights for all kinds of biased reasons. They are quick to say that children do best with and need two parents, but then in divorce, they routinely leave children with one parent and a visitor without significant parenting ability in their lives. They strip the child of the security, safety, and stability that each fit parent provides. They try to force parents to conform to a court's idea of a perfect parent or deprive the family of their parental rights and authority, punishing the children for the parent's perceived flaws. Flaws that otherwise were part of that child's life, that the child was accustomed to. When the court interferes, they make that child's parents into strangers and forever destroy and steal all that made that child what they are; forever altering the uniqueness and strengths that child would have acquired through their continued association with both parents.

    This amendment serves to protect the uniqueness of parent's

## Protecting Parent-Child Bonds

personalities and choices in how they choose to raise their child despite individual opinions, dislikes, or biases of the judge. This amendment protects each parent from being bullied, harassed, terrorized, or forced into being the parent that someone else chooses for him or her. This amendment protects parents from being told by their children what type of parent they should be in order to continue with the "privilege" of having their child in their life after the divorce court places the child in a dominate position. Parenting is NOT a "privilege" it is a natural right. This amendment puts a stop to this massive social experiment where a small number of divorce court judges are allowed to have profound control over how a large number of our children are raised.

In cases other than divorce, child protective agencies are known to routinely violate the constitutional rights of parents. As recently as this year Federal Appellate Courts have ruled that child protective agencies violated the Fourth Amendment by entering a parent's home, searching the parent's home, and interviewing the parent's children all under threat of taking their children through unconstitutional means. The Appellate Courts have made clear that there is NO "best interests" exemption to the US Constitution and yet these agencies in many states continue their unconstitutional practices. States routinely, daily, violate the constitutional rights of parents and children in divorce.

States simply do not live up to their professed state interest in protecting the parent-child bond and that children need two fit parents. Nor do they live up to their duty to protect the natural rights of both parents equally and individually. There is an epidemic of motherless and fatherless children, that scientists are saying clearly hurts children. This happens not because these parents don't want to be parents, but because the State in divorce typicaly makes it impossible for them to be parents.

As we are writing this, Tom Cruise is suing a tabloid for claiming that he abandoned his child. This tabloid tried to accuse him of abandoning her rather than run a story on how the divorce courts limited him and stripped the child of her equal association with both parents. If they find the limited contact that he is allowed to have with his daughter to be abandonment, they should be ques-

## Chapter 4 — THE FITNESS CLAUSE

tioning the courts as to why they have unconstitutionally deprived this child of her father instead of attacking the parent. This is a problem in our culture. We would rather attack parents than correct a corrupt family law culture.

States often set up the most arbitrary reasons for depriving children of two fit parents. By far the most used excuse is divorce. Somehow, the states believe that when two parents get divorced that the State is granted a right and a duty to take over all decision making for the child. Some states are so nuts in this area that they even give divorce courts authority to take over decision making for the adults as well—Florida, for instance, gives divorce courts this statutory authority without restriction even though it is clearly unconstitutional; Statute 61.052 "...the court may...Take such other action as may be in the best interest of the parties and the minor child of the marriage."

Some states will deprive fit parents of their rights for all kinds of reasons that are not necessarily good for the children. Then after they take the children they apply a lesser standard of care to themselves than they applied to take the children from the parents in the first place. They hold parents to higher standards of care than they hold the State and often these children end up neglected, abused, molested, raped, and even murdered under state control.

States have historically taken children from otherwise fit parents simply for moral reasons. In the past parents lost their children for not living up to purely religious standards. Parents are supposed to have a First Amendment right to educate their children in their own moral beliefs and values, regardless of the majority belief, but that is not always applied.

Our book *"NOT In the Child's Best Interest"*, discusses a 1974 case where an Appellate Court said that the father had parental rights but that those rights could be denied because he was a politically active homosexual and educated his children in his politics. This would hopefully not be tolerated today but it was done then, and homosexuality was widely considered illegal. Today, parents often lose their children for possession of minor amounts of minor illegal drugs without any evidence that they have harmed their

## Protecting Parent-Child Bonds

child at all or that they did anything in the presence of the child. If this is the standard then a parent can lose their child for jay walking.

Very often, the courts say that because the parents can't agree to something like a single bedtime for the child, the mere fact that they disagree is grounds for the Court to deprive one or the other of their constitutionally protected right to choose for themselves and for their child.

Adults have been using drugs and raising children for the entire history of our species, thousands of years, while the practice of making drugs illegal isn't even 100 years old. Many parents are functioning alcoholics and are allowed to raise their children even when they drink in front of their children. If a parent uses any kind of "illegal" drug even if the drug is less harmful than alcohol and they don't do it in front of the children, State's still use this as an excuse to remove children.

Meanwhile, parents who are in jail for other crimes against people, even violent crimes, are generally allowed to keep their parental rights. O. J. Simpson, for instance, was allowed to raise his children, but only because his ex-wife was murdered and therefore not alive to challenge custody in divorce court.

This is one of the many reasons why we insist on the standard of "clear and present danger." While it is perfectly acceptable to have criminal punishment for criminal behavior, it is NOT acceptable to deprive a child of a fit parent based on adult behavior unrelated to the health, welfare, and safety of the child. Keep in mind that a long prison sentence would make a parent unable to care for the child and therefore subject to lose their parental rights.

In the Fitness Clause, we make parental unfitness the only way to deprive a parent of their parental rights. Further, we clearly define the four conditions under which unfitness may be defined. We also make clear that parents MUST be presumed to be fit unless proven otherwise by the State under one of the listed conditions. This is nothing less than the right of innocence until guilt is proven, a bedrock principle of our free nation.

## Chapter 4 — THE FITNESS CLAUSE

The first of the four listed conditions is that the parent must have placed the child in clear and present danger as a direct result of that parent's decisions. There are several important issues addressed in this clause. First, the Tennessee Supreme Court in Hawk v. Hawk, (1993), went to great lengths to ensure the rights of parents in intact nuclear families, but then specifically exempted divorced parents. The twisted logic evident here was that the process of divorcing is so harmful to the children that the State MUST step in and take over. They didn't even consider that the States that make the divorce laws and the courts that carry them out create the difficulty of the divorce process NOT the parents.

They never even considered that if the rights of both parents to be parents were protected equally there would be no reason to fight in court over custody, no reason to pay attorneys for custody battles, and no reason to pay mental health professionals to violate Fourth and Fifth Amendment rights. They never once considered that billions of dollars are flowing to their "professional associates" at these children's expense. Or did they? Are those billions of dollars the real reason this travesty continues?

It is the very act of intervening with a winner-take-all system that leaves children with one parent and one visitor following divorce that is harmful in a child's life. By their logic, when a parent dies the State should be stepping in and taking over because the harm that a parent's death has on the child.

This type of twisted reasoning is found in almost every State as they are dead-set on protecting their power to interfere with divorcing parents' rights. They don't do this when a parent dies because there usually isn't a pocketbook to dig into and there is no longer a fundamental bias against widows and widowers, although there once was and this was once used as an excuse to take children.

For this reason specifically, we have used the term "clear and present danger" to clearly scope the type of harm that must exist before the state may intervene. This term has a much stronger legal definition than the term "harm" which is wide open to a lowered and broader interpretation.

## Protecting Parent-Child Bonds

Second, we added the requirement that the clear and present danger to the child MUST come directly from a parent's decision. We have read too many cases of child protective services (CPS) using the widest possible definition of harm to remove children; and in way too many instances that harm was NOT caused in any way by the parents.

In one specific example, a mother was stalked and violently, physically assaulted by a former boyfriend who went to jail. CPS then sought to remove her child because of the potential harm to be caused by the boyfriend getting out of jail and assaulting her again, even though the mother took great pains to protect herself and her child from that eventuality.

Here you have CPS punishing a victim of criminal assault by taking away her child because she was assaulted. These kinds of conditions are completely unacceptable and have become way too common in divorce and are to be absolutely prohibited by this Amendment.

Children should only be removed from parents based on decisions and actions that the parent is directly responsible for, unless otherwise covered in this Amendment. Seeking a divorce from a spouse is NOT and can-NOT be a harm of this type; even if considered harmful in general, the harm is directly caused by the state mandated process and not the parents. Further, it is not a type of harm that the State may properly protect a child from.

The second of the four listed conditions is if the parent is unable to care for the child. There are many temporary conditions where this might happen. One is where a parent becomes ill and for the duration of the illness they are unable to care for their child. Another is where a parent in the military is required to serve where children aren't allowed. These temporary even if long-term deployments may not be used to deprive the parent or the child of their constitutional parental rights.

Many divorce courts have permanently deprived service members of their parental rights for this reason, even when that parent took great care to provide fit surrogate care for the child.

## Chapter 4 — THE FITNESS CLAUSE

The hypocrisy in this is that married parents' may exercise their right to send their child to military school or boarding school where they spend prolonged periods of time away from the child and it is never questioned, so long as they continue to be married and to agree.

Sometimes, people, rightfully or wrongfully, are arrested and spend a considerable amount of time in jail for issues having absolutely nothing to do with their child's care; these people should NOT permanently lose their children. It is appropriate for the State in these circumstances to step in as parent of last resort and temporarily ensure that the children are adequately cared for until the parent is able to do so once again.

The third of the four conditions is one where the State has substantial latitude still to ensure that minimum standards of health and safety are maintained for children if applied to everyone equally. Some parents simply are unwilling to do what it takes to meet the minimum needs of their children and the children are clearly better off with alternative arrangements. In these cases, where the state proves its case, it is appropriate for the State to assume responsibility for the children. The bar, however, must be the same for all parents and cannot be based on individual personal bias or personal beliefs or an altered standard because a parent is going through divorce.

The fourth condition is for parents who probably would be willing and able, sometimes at great hardship, to care for their children but for whatever reason they believe that their children would be better off with another. These parents may waive their rights to their children and those children many times are put up for adoption.

Teenage pregnancy is a typical scenario where a mother and father waive their rights to a child so that adults who are better situated to care for that child can raise the child. These situations can include great love and commitment to the child by the natural parents who in a difficult situation place what they want for their child over what they can provide for them, and provide a home for the child that they consider better situated.

## Protecting Parent-Child Bonds

The important concept in this condition is that the waiver must be a knowing, intelligent waiver free from coercion. This means that the parent MUST clearly understand all of their rights and responsibilities and be of sound mind to make the decision. Requiring parents to sign this waiver an hour after a child is delivered would clearly violate this provision as both a form of coercion and a situation where their cognitive ability to knowingly waive the right is potentially impaired. Divorce court judges should also be prohibited from using their immense State power to intimidate parents into giving in to the other parent and surrendering their parental rights.

What happens today in divorce is that parents give away their parental rights without knowing it. This is done by their attorneys who draw up divorce pleadings that make no reference to constitutional fundamental rights but that ask the judge to decide the child's fate based on the judge's personal beliefs and biased determination of the child's best interests.

Most parents have no idea that the Supreme Court has clearly said that fit parents are the appropriate parties to make determinations of their child's best interest and not a judge, even if that judge feels they can make a better decision. Attorneys routinely fail to inform parents of their constitutional rights, and as a result, those parents unintentionally forfeit their rights.

This Amendment is designed to stop that kind of underhanded or thoughtless legal maneuvering and make it illegal under any conditions. A parent MUST know their rights and clearly know that they are giving up those rights before any waiver of parental rights can have the force of law under this Amendment. This Amendment will stop the massive and unconscionable transfer of wealth from children to attorneys and mental health professionals simply because their parents divorced. Children of divorce suffer enough without being impoverished by the very system that claims to protect them.

Some people will argue that limiting the State's authority to these four conditions is too restrictive. However, the people inherently restrict State authority in the first place and we embodied

## Chapter 4 — THE FITNESS CLAUSE

this restriction in the U.S. Constitution. We believe that the States have demonstrated the need for clear restriction. And, we believe, that these conditions leave adequate room for laws that protect children where strict scrutiny is applied.

One area of law making ability is in defining the term "minimum basic needs." It is clear that the minimum basic needs of a child two hundred years ago were much less than what we would apply today. The State is free to legislate minimum educational needs, minimum health care needs, and minimum health and safety needs, to name a few, so long as they meet the strict scrutiny test and are equally applied to all parents regardless of marital status or of changes in marital status. There must be one and only one standard by which all parents are measured.

By making the statement that "the state must prove" these conditions, it should be clear that only a state action against a parent is sufficient to deprive a parent of their rights. This is a direct response to State's hiding the very nature of divorce proceedings today. Today State's claim that in divorce proceedings they are facilitating a civil claim between parents, however, NO parent has a constitutional, legal, or equitable claim on the other parent's fundamental constitutional parental rights or to destroy, intervene in, or diminish the parent-child bond between the other parent and their child. If they have no claim then there cannot be a civil dispute between them.

What is actually happening today is that States are using their power (not constitutional authority but raw power) to unconstitutionally punish parents in divorce by depriving them of fundamental liberty interests; using the private civil action as a cover to confuse parents into believing that the state's unconstitutional acts are appropriate; and to do so without proper due process safeguards.

It's simply cheaper and easier for the State to hide their unconstitutional practice of depriving divorcing parents of rights and collect Title IV D payments under the label of "civil action between parents." These bad practices are encouraged and perpetuated by the State based on pure bias and prejudice against divorcing parents pushed along by the profit motive.

The reason this is insidious is that by confusing the issue in this way, the state is able to deprive parents of their rights using a much lesser standard of proof and without being required to make specific claims in writing against the parent. It also saves the State from being required to give proper notice of charges to which the parent can properly respond and defend. The State is then able to leverage the services of a biased prosecutor in the form of the other parent's attorney, at no cost to the State, to deprive parents of their rights in a wholesale manner. They do this without applying any of the checks and balances provided in our criminal and quasi-criminal system of justice that would normally be required to deprive someone of fundamental rights.

Once this is done, child support can naturally be awarded, and the federal government then pays the State through Title IV D of the Social Security Act. If rights are unevenly distributed and more time is given to one parent than the other then an excellent smokescreen is created to provide cover for awarding child support that is nothing less than denying that parent the right and ability to care for their own child directly. That parent is forever deprived of the meaningful parent-child interaction that derives directly from this care.

While it is hard for most people to argue against child support under these terms, we offer an alternative view. The right to care for your child is a fundamental constitutional right. This means that you have the right to directly care for the child, and not be forced to pay someone else to do so. Unless a parent is unwilling to equally care for their child directly, there is absolutely no justification for the State forcing them to pay the other parent.

The States also do this today under civil actions between the State and parents through their "child protective services." These agencies by any measure are completely out of control and too often deprive fit parents of their rights over nothing more than disagreements over parenting styles. Most of these agencies act without any clear bar for their interventions. They become supremely arrogant and violate rights at every turn because they

## Chapter 4 — THE FITNESS CLAUSE

believe that they are protecting children or sometimes simply because they have the power. This Amendment clearly sets the bar for intervention and ensures that the State cannot move that bar to suit its whims.

Only by clearly articulating the conditions under which parental rights may be properly deprived and properly labeling state deprivations as such can we stop the bias driven practices that are so horribly destructive to legitimate parent-child bonds. We must finally put a stop to these inhuman practices that occur every day in every State in this nation.

# Chapter 5

## THE RIGHTS OF FIT PARENTS

Within the Fitness Clause are four enumerated sub-clauses that are very specific about some of the rights fit parents have. The key word here is "some." There are those who believe that if the right isn't written down that it doesn't exist. The following statement is explicitly for those people.

> THIS IS NOT AN EXCLUSIVE LIST AND MORE SUBSTANTIVE PARENTAL RIGHTS MAY NEED TO BE SPECIFICALLY PROTECTED BASED ON THE ACTIONS OF THE STATES TO CONTINUE INTERVENING IN PARENTAL RIGHTS. THIS NEEDS TO BE VERY CLEAR FOR THOSE WHO DO NOT BELIEVE IN SUBSTANTIVE RIGHTS, FIT PARENTS HAVE MORE RIGHTS THAN ARE LISTED HERE.

The following points are to clarify some of the boundaries that the State may NOT cross.

**The first sub-clause clarifies that:**

*(1) Fit parents are entrusted by nature or the State with determining the best interests of their minor child and must be assumed to be acting in their child's best interests unless proven unfit.*

Based on more than 100 years of states depriving fit par-

## Protecting Parent-Child Bonds

ents of their rights under the Fourteenth Amendment, we feel it is absolutely essential that we make a clear statement regarding the child's best interests and who is to determine what those best interests are. There is nobody better positioned than a fit parent to know their child, to know the needs of their child, and to care about and make decisions regarding what is best for that child. Even marginal parents are better than State care.

Nobody from the state, not mental health care workers, not attorneys, not other experts, not the judge, and not even the other parent has a right to interfere with a fit parent's right to determine best interest during their equal time with their child. Fitness as a parent means that you are free to raise your child as you see fit without anybody second-guessing your decisions.

This responsibility comes naturally to natural parents and is welcomed by legal parents who in becoming legal parents agree to take on this responsibility. These people, the parents, are the best people to decide for and care for their own children.

Courts and judges only get a tiny sliver of information filtered through countless rules, regulations, and court practices. They handle many hundreds of cases every year and they have NO personal vested interest in anybody's child except their own. Judges carry moral, religious, political, and secular biases that enter into any decision they make, and, when they act in their official capacity with nearly unlimited discretion, these biases become State biases imposed arbitrarily on the family and the child. Proper implementation of parental rights greatly reduces the probability that these personal beliefs, biases, or any other influences outside the Constitution will even come into play or become a part of the judge's decision making process.

There are international trends to protect children's rights that seem to ignore any ability of the child to exercise those rights or to make competent decisions regarding their own best interests. There is an international treaty that has been before the Senate and is scheduled to be before the Senate again this year for ratification. It proposes to protect children by making the determination of the child's best interest a political issue for the State to

## Chapter 5 — THE RIGHTS OF FIT PARENTS

decide. While the motives behind these efforts may be good, its effect can be as harmful to a child as would be handing them a loaded gun and telling them to go play.

This sub-clause makes clear that we support the rights of children while at the same time we recognize that children do not have the capacity to exercise those rights effectively. Someone must hold those rights in trust for that child. For this reason and more we make clear that "fit parents determine a child's best interests." We feel that this is best for children and also meets the intent of international efforts to protect children; efforts that we support under this condition. Children have rights that are best protected by fit parents holding those rights in trust, not politicians, state agencies, judges or other state actors.

This sub-clause states where the authority to act in the child's best interest comes from. For natural parents, the authority comes from natural law and is specifically protected by this Amendment. For parents established by law, the authority comes from the U.S. Constitution generally and through this Amendment to that Constitution specifically.

Each parent has this authority as a protected right 100% of the time and those rights are equal between natural parents. These rights do not disappear in a marriage and do not attach to the marriage. These rights remain 100% for both parents regardless of whether or not they are going through a divorce.

Each parent's ability to exercise this right is relative to his or her custody and possession time with the child. Therefore, by reducing a parent's time to less than equal when they get divorced, the state is depriving one parent of their ability to exercise their full natural rights.

Under this Amendment, whichever parent has care, custody, control, and possession of the child at any point in time has the authority to act in the child's best interest during that time and is primary during that time in that capacity so long as their action doesn't deprive the other parent of rights.

## Protecting Parent-Child Bonds

There are situations where this authority can interfere with another parents' ability to exercise their rights during their time, for instance determining geographically where the child will live, which school they will attend, and what discretionary invasive medical procedures the child may receive. These are singular decisions that can't generally be changed during each possession period.

For those limited types of situations where rights are in conflict and the parents can NOT agree and the right cannot be split equally, then the Court may properly decide just those narrow issues, under strict scrutiny conditions. In NO instance does the State have "broad" discretion to determine a child's best interests over the determination of a fit parent, even where two fit parents disagree.

The state today, under Supreme Court interpretation of the Constitution, may certainly regulate the exercise of protected private decisions, so long as that regulation is NOT unduly burdensome on the right to make those decisions. For this reason, the State may require parents to formally establish the rules under which they will jointly exercise these rights and how they will resolve disagreements. Many states define these types of agreements as "parenting plans."

The only route for the State to assume broad discretion to determine a child's best interests is if a parent is determined to be unfit either permanently or temporarily and where probable cause exists to believe that a child is being placed in clear and present danger.

In those situations, where the State believes that a child is in clear and present danger, the State may take temporary action to protect the child but must then move with all haste to prove that harm or to restore the parent and child to each other. It is currently the state's duty to prove their action was justified and it should remain so and be enforced.

Any action by the State to deprive a parent of rights to their child MUST be seen as a punishment for some claimed act by the

## Chapter 5 — THE RIGHTS OF FIT PARENTS

parent and must be proven in a quasi-criminal proceeding properly labeled as an action by the State against a parent. Regardless of whether the action by the state is perpetrated "in the child's best interests", it is a punishment and must be regarded as a punishment. The Supreme Court has ruled that any deprivation of a fundamental liberty is a punishment.

Nothing in this Amendment should have any effect on any Court interpretation of the privacy rights of women that give rise to the "right to abortion" nor should it have any effect on Court interpretation that determines when and how a child must notify parents of their intent to have an abortion. Once the child is determined to have rights that must be protected then the parent-child bond must also be protected.

While we respect both sides of the abortion debate, we also respect the political and judicial processes by which these issues are being determined. Nothing in this Amendment is intended to impact that process in any way. For instance, this Amendment does not mention when children's rights are recognized as distinctly separate from the mother's right nor does it mention anything about when a child's right to decide for themselves overrides that of the parents.

This last statement requires clarification so that nobody tries to wedge this issue into the debate. The clarification is that under no condition is the State permitted to allow the child to choose between two fit parents. While those parents are fit, they share the rights equally to parent the child until the child reaches the age of majority within the rules set for all parents equally regarding the transition of children from minority to majority.

**The Second sub-clause clarifies that:**

*(2) Each fit parent has the equal right and duty to direct and control their minor child's education, to include educating the minor child through personal example, which arises through routine parenting of the child. The child has a right to receive education from each parent equally. These rights*

*are among the penumbra of individual First Amendment rights.*

This sub-clause covers ground that the US Supreme Court has covered to some depth and its basis is found in the First Amendment and the Fourteenth Amendment. The Supreme Court has made clear that parents have a right to educate their children in the moral, religious, and civic values of their choice. However, the States have seen fit to deny this equal right to parents in divorce and have so far gotten away with it. The State does this today by depriving one parent of equal time with the child.

The word "routine" is not to be construed as a word to support status quo and is not to be construed to mean that less than equal time is appropriate because the parent doesn't exercise equal time.

We believe that every child benefits from parents who care about that child's education and preparation for life. The views of that parent are NOT generally subject to censure by the state or the other parent. We, and the Supreme Court see this as a duty of parents to ensure that their child is prepared to be a productive member of society. Children benefit from a wide range of exposure to values and knowledge through everyday interactions where parents may not even realize that children are learning from and that exposure should not be arbitrarily denied the child by the courts. Each parent, individually, gets to determine what their child is exposed to during their time under equally applicable laws.

Anytime a court chooses one parent over the other and denies a fit parent equal time with their child, that court is denying the child the opportunity to learn by example from that parent through the normal and routine activities of everyday life. When a judge makes these decisions they are enforcing their own personal moral, religious, and civic values as an exercise of state power. They are in effect, violating the First Amendment which provides that the State may not make laws regulating religion or denying free speech or free association.

A very small group of very powerful judges are shaping and

## Chapter 5 — THE RIGHTS OF FIT PARENTS

improperly influencing an ever increasing number of children's moral, civic, and religious educations based on their own personal biases. Can we really afford to have this level of bias forcibly applied to our children? Can we really afford to have the beliefs of such a small group of people to have such a profound effect on our children and destroy the full potential of possible future leaders of our country? Is this really the kind of social engineering that we are prepared to tolerate in this country?

The clarification in this sub-clause is intended to strengthen the relationship between First Amendment principles and the protection of parent-child bonds. It is intended to raise the care given to the protection of these bonds to be equal with First Amendment protections. It is intended to ensure the opportunity of equal parenting time for fit parents regardless of marital status or changes in marital status.

What this clarification is not intended to do is to give individual parents control over our public schools. States can and should determine the minimum education standards that children receive and states should direct the public school systems for the common good. However, the States are currently forbidden to force all students into public education and that is how it should remain.

So long as fit parents meet the minimum state standards of education those parents should remain free to educate their children as they see fit, in the environment which they see fit, and to whatever higher standard they see fit.

This Amendment is not intended to directly impact any existing Court opinions regarding the line drawn between parent's rights and the rights of the States to manage the public schools.

Parents remain free to educate their children themselves or through a third party, either an individual or an organization of their choice so long as they meet the minimum state standards for education. These minimum standards must be broadly applicable and not designed to unduly burden this right in any way.

## Protecting Parent-Child Bonds
**The third sub-clause clarifies that:**

*(3) Fit parents hold equal rights and duties in the care, custody, control, and physical possession of the minor child. Any conflict between these rights must be resolved in as equal a manner as possible.*

Every State at some point in their recent history and most as of this writing regularly deny the equal rights of fit parents particularly in divorce, and also where parents are never married. The states regularly exclude possession time with the child as being included in protected rights of both parents equally. The Rights of parents and of children are NOT and can NOT be vested in the marriage. They are individual in nature and the privacy rights of families are grounded in the family relationship between each parent and each child individually. It is the individual parent-child bond between each parent and each child that is to be protected first and primarily by this Amendment.

These rights are held in full by each parent and are always in conflict. Marriage provides a convenient means of managing these conflicts that primarily leaves the parents free from government intrusion into how they allocate these rights between each other on a day-by-day or even moment-by-moment basis.

Marriage is generally a good mechanism for this purpose and has been supported by governments since time immemorial, even when the marital arrangement was less than equal. Today, in America, marital arrangements are between equal people with equal legal rights and neither party to the marriage is given any superior or inferior rights upon granting of the marriage.

Divorce or the lack of marriage does NOT and can NOT diminish the rights of either parent nor can it trigger the State's *parens patriae* interests beyond a non-burdensome administrative intervention. There simply is NO legal relationship between the marriage and the rights of the parents.

Neither divorce nor conflict between parents grants the State

## Chapter 5 — THE RIGHTS OF FIT PARENTS

or any court authority to deny, restrict, or infringe upon any parental right except under the terms of strict scrutiny, where the State has proven a compelling state interest, has crafted a narrowly tailored law in support of that interest, and where the law and court rulings have the least restrictive impact on the rights being infringed as is possible, and are equally applied to all parents regardless of whether they are married, going through divorce, single, or widowed. Further, the law is and will always be presumed unconstitutional until proven otherwise by the State.

What this leaves for the State and for Divorce Courts is an administrative role where the extent of their authority to act in or determine the child's best interests is to require the parties to create an enforceable parenting plan that sets out the parents equal rights and how they plan to exercise those rights. The parents of their own volition may choose to exercise less than 100% of their rights without losing those rights. For instance one parent may prefer to work and provide financially, even in divorce, if the other parent cares for the child in an agreed manner.

This parent should be allowed at any time to change to a different caregiver whenever they decide the other parent no longer cares for the child during their time as they choose. Neither parent should be forced into deprivation of their rights just because they assign another person to care for their child unless their assignment has reached the definition of abandonment applied to all parents equally.

This does not preclude a finding of unfitness for abandonment of the child from willfully refusing to care for and support the child. Most rights come with responsibilities; parental rights come with massive responsibilities. Failure to attend to those responsibilities consistently over time is a legitimate basis under this Amendment to lose parental rights. Any deprivation or taking of rights must be through a proper termination hearing.

The Supreme Court has already ruled many times that parents have a right to the care, custody, and control of their children. They have not to our knowledge specifically called out possession except for reference to New York definitions of custody which in-

## Protecting Parent-Child Bonds

clude possession. We believe that possession time is to be found in both the terms *"custody"* and *"control."*

The Court's latest statement on this issue comes after they cited a long history of support for parental rights, *"In light of this extensive precedent, it cannot now be doubted that the Due Process Clause of the Fourteenth Amendment protects the fundamental right of parents to make decisions concerning the care, custody, and control of their children."*

Even with this clear statement from the highest Court in the land, States continue to deny fit parents the ability to exercise these rights every day in every state. It is precisely because the States have continued to thumb their noses at the Constitution and Supreme Court opinions that we feel the need to demand a strongly worded constitutional amendment that clearly protects all parents and children, even those going through divorce. Perhaps, the mere threat of this Amendment passing will prompt states to action but if it doesn't then the Amendment itself will clarify the issues beyond the States' abilities to befuddle.

State Courts have found every illogical and irrational excuse possible to get around the basic fact that they are depriving fit parents of their fundamental constitutional rights based on nothing more than bias and prejudice directed at divorcing parents. The Divorce Courts would have us believe that fit parents who act in their child's best interests within the marriage framework somehow become unfit and do not act in their child's best interests simply because they choose to end a marriage and no longer get along with the other parent and cannot come to agreement. The State Courts would have you believe that your parental rights are based on your marriage even though single-never-married parents seem to have parental rights just fine without a marriage.

The Courts would have you believe that because the parents don't agree that the State MUST take over all rights over the child and then grant them back to their favored parent. The reality is that many married parents don't get along, many married parents have different religions, many married parents fight and yet somehow if they stay married, no matter how dysfunctional, those

## Chapter 5 — THE RIGHTS OF FIT PARENTS

parents get to keep their rights and, no matter how functional, divorced parents are forced to give up their rights the moment divorce is filed. This is fundamentally unequal treatment under the law of persons who are similarly situated regarding the source of their parental rights and their fitness to exercise those parental rights.

The Divorce Courts like to blame parents for fighting over their children and yet some states refuse to allow judges to sign orders stating that parents have equal rights and equal possession time. They are literally saying to each parent, "We are going to take from one of you what is most important in your life and give it to the other person. Also, we are going to make you pay for the privilege of suffering this loss. Oh and by the way, if you fight this as being inherently unfair, unconstitutional, and immoral we will blame you for being a bad parent and accuse you of not putting your child's interests first.

How dare you, as a parent, fight the all-powerful divorce court judge? How dare you claim that you know better than the state what is best for your child? How dare you fight to keep the State from taking your child from you?" How dare you not agree with the other parent?

This sub-clause is designed to state with as much clarity and exactitude as possible that the State may NOT take these rights from fit parents even when fit parents divorce and disagree over their children. Divorce is NOT and can NEVER be the basis for denial of parental rights or destruction of parent-child bonds.

Depriving one parent over the other is a denial even when it is only seen as a deprivation and not a termination. That is one of the excuses that states have used to avoid having to apply the proper level of scrutiny and due process. They say that depriving a parent does not warrant the same high level of due process as terminating a parent altogether. This amendment should make clear that all deprivations are violations that must meet the Strict Scrutiny test and that even deprivations can be just as harmful and damaging as wrongful termination.

## Protecting Parent-Child Bonds

When a parent's authority is reduced, the safety and security that the child feels with that parent is destroyed. This hurts children and this amendment is meant to protect children from this harm and loss.

Many people believe that it isn't possible for two parents who disagree to effectively parent their child and that the State must take over. We know for a fact that this belief is false because we live it every day.

The family courts also regularly restrict what a parent can say to their child and say publicly. Many people today still believe it to be perfectly all right for people to be jailed for what they say regardless of what the Constitution says. Still today all over this country police write citations to people for nothing more than verbally expressing themselves.

We have helped two different people challenge these citations in the last 5 years and prevail. One of us was even threatened by a Captain of police, a lieutenant of police, and several officers in the lobby of our police station for protected free speech, a curse word, whispered between two friends. One of us was threatened with arrest for using a curse word and the Captain even said "I would love to meet you in a dark alley sometime." This happened because we disagreed with the police violating our constitutional rights and we were legally and calmly collecting public records to prove that they had done so, records that they had failed to provide in violation of State and Federal law.

We were able to fight these injustices and win precisely because these freedoms are documented in a constitutional amendment. If they were only found in Supreme Court opinions as parental rights are today it would have been much more difficult to fight.

The point is that when we have fundamental constitutional rights it becomes the State's duty to prove that it has sufficient enough public need to interfere with those rights and even then its ability to interfere is severely restricted. If the State can't prove clear and present danger to a child then the State has NO business

## Chapter 5 — THE RIGHTS OF FIT PARENTS

interfering with the rights of fit parents to raise their child as they see fit even when those parents disagree.

The State can't just assume you are a criminal and throw you in jail or search your house without a warrant. Neither, can they take your parental rights just because they assume you aren't caring for your child appropriately. It is the State's responsibility to prove these things before taking action. It is the State's responsibility to hold the proper hearing with the proper pleadings before they proceed. Otherwise their actions are unconstitutional, illegal, and without any lawful justification.

**The fourth sub-clause verifies that:**

*(4) Fit parents may entrust certain of these rights to others as they see fit without forfeiting their rights.*

Our nation has a long and rich history of parents sending their children to boarding schools such as college preparatory schools or military schools. Even though this trend has lessened in recent years, the tradition is nevertheless alive. Even as we write this, there is an interstate billboard advertising the value of a particular military boarding school just a few miles from our home stating what kind of parent sends their child to a military school, "a proud one." At least one of our immediate friends attended such a school.

Many parents have historically, and still do today, arrange for other relatives to care for their children when they go through hard times, and for many other equally valid reasons, because they believe that their child may be better off during a temporary period in the care of a relative. This is a supreme example of fit parents placing the needs of their children before their own desires, an act that the State may not constitutionally compel.

Many parents experience hardships or take on obligations to their nation through military service and are required to spend long periods of time away from their children. Several of our

## Protecting Parent-Child Bonds

greatest Founding Fathers had to entrust the care and upbringing of their children to others for significant periods of time while they served their nation. It was for them unthinkable that they might lose rights to their children as a result of their service.

Franklin and Jefferson both spent years abroad as ambassadors for our country and much of that time was spent with their children in America. Neither would support the idea that this separation entitles the State to take over control of their children.

We have been a country at war for more than a decade now. We have many thousands of parents who have had to serve overseas for a year or more and many have done this multiple times. Many of those parents lost their children to the divorce courts. Not because they were unfit parents but because they served their country and protected all of us from foreign threats to our security. They were repaid for their service by the divorce courts with losing their parental rights.

This sub-clause is intended to ensure that parents, American service members, divorcing parents and others, will NEVER be subject to losing their rights simply because they were faced with a situation or made a choice for their children to be cared for by others. So long as parents provide for the minimum basic needs of their children directly or indirectly, and place their children in competent hands, they should NOT lose their rights as parents no matter the duration or the reason for the separation.

We hope to create a condition where there is never again an American service member who comes home from extended service only to find they have lost the very thing they were away fighting to protect. We hope to send a very strong signal to Divorce Courts throughout this nation that this dishonorable conduct on their part MUST come to an end.

(In full disclosure: One of us served in both the U.S. Marine Corps. and the U.S. Army)

# Chapter 6

## THE NATURAL RIGHTS CLAUSE

> *3. The rights of natural (biological) parents are neither established nor granted by the State but are self-evident rights that shall be protected by the State and by this Amendment. The State may create legal parents where that creation does not unduly burden the rights of natural parents without their consent to the burden. Once established, except where specifically limited, legal parents are granted protection under this Amendment.*

This clause is intended to clarify the nature of parental rights. It should be forever clear from this clause that States do NOT grant rights to natural parents. Those rights are among the rights spoken of in our Declaration of Independence as rights that are self-evident. Benjamin Franklin proposed this specific wording and it is intended to say that these are natural rights that come before government and that protection of these rights is the reason we created our governments in the first place.

It is way too common for those with government power to take the view that all rights are held by the government and then granted to individuals as the government sees fit. THIS IS ABSOLUTELY NOT THE CASE AND SHOULD BE EMPHATICALLY DEMONSTRATED HERE. It is the State's responsibility to the people to protect the rights of the people. This is precisely why governments were formed and why people allow themselves to be governed.

There are multiple instances where people other than natural

## Protecting Parent-Child Bonds

parents need the protection of parental rights either partially or in full. For instance step-parents often share a significant burden of parenting their step-children. While we do NOT propose giving step-parents direct or full rights, they do need the authority to parent the children under their care.

We believe that this authority does not come directly from the marriage but indirectly through the natural parent. The step-parent is and should be vested with parental authority only as the natural parent's agent. Except in special circumstances established over long periods of care, step-parents should not be personally vested with these rights over either of the natural parents or other fully vested legal parents.

There is certainly room within this Amendment for step-parents (for instance) who have developed and nurtured parent-child bonds to have rights within the scope of their spouse's rights and that these rights may be respected and protected even after the death of their spouse, the natural parent. Where a step-parent has such a bond developed over a long period of time, that bond deserves protection and that protection is not intended to be prohibited within this amendment.

The U.S. Supreme Court has some case history established on the threshold of when and how a non-parent can establish parent-child bonds over time and establish a case for parental rights. We do not seek to end that tradition here but to ensure that the natural and fully vested legal parents are protected before third parties can assert parental rights.

We do want to assert a difference with how the Supreme Court currently recognizes the rights of natural fathers which is not automatic and requires certain actions on the part of the natural father for those rights to be recognized. We believe this is a travesty. Both natural parents are and should be fully vested with natural rights to their children. No natural parent should ever have to "establish" their rights because that makes a mockery of the very concept of natural rights and it allows women to hide children from fathers to block their rights.

## Chapter 6 — THE NATURAL RIGHTS CLAUSE

Establishing rights is different from establishing paternity. No State should ever be allowed to block a potential natural parent from asserting their paternity. Once paternity is established the natural rights must be respected and protected.

In cases where a natural father knows about their child they should be allowed to exercise their parental rights fully and equally without hindrance from the other parent or the government. If either parent knowingly fails to provide for the minimum basic needs of their child then they can be found unfit just like any other natural or legal parent. Natural parents are vested at birth with parental rights. Only if they knowingly fail to accept those rights and the associated duties, or meet the other conditions of this Amendment, can they then be stripped of those rights.

No natural parent should ever be long deprived of the ability to exercise their rights except upon being found unfit and the State should only intervene when the parent is unable to care for the child or when the parent is being formally investigated and charged with causing clear and present danger to the child. Just to be clear, willfully neglecting the minimum basic needs of a child or leaving the child without age appropriate care can be considered putting that child in clear and present danger.

People generally have a fundamental right to be free from constraint but the State can under certain circumstances constrain a person for a period of time before and after they are convicted of any crime. There are many limitations on this State power. The State has a similar power to temporarily separate a parent and child but the limitations on this power should be similar to that of restricting the accused criminal's movement. The State always bears the burden of proof for its actions to deprive parental rights.

Marriage is a well-respected tradition that provides people and society with many benefits. While the State may choose to define legal parents as a result of children born to a marriage, those legal rights do not supersede those of a natural fit parent. The extent of the rights of that legal parent should come only from their spouse's equal share of rights.

## Protecting Parent-Child Bonds

For instance, if a married woman should become pregnant from a man other than her husband, the natural parents have equal rights. If the husband is granted legal rights to the child then the ability to exercise those rights can never lessen the equal ability of the natural father to exercise his rights, they can only lessen the ability of the natural mother to exercise her rights. The implementation details of this kind of increasingly common situation are left to the discretion of the State legislatures.

Natural parents should never be prohibited from entering into an arrangement where there are more than two parents each with equal rights. It is only that no fit natural parent should ever be forced into such a situation.

These statements fly directly in the face of a relatively recent Supreme Court opinion where a natural father was prevented from having any rights at all to his child because the woman to whom the child was born was married and the State automatically makes the husband the father and leaves the natural father no path to assert paternity. We strongly disagree with this opinion as it makes a mockery of the very idea of natural rights. No natural parent should ever be denied opportunity to assert paternity under this amendment.

The way the Supreme Court currently but incorrectly provides recognition for father's rights is what allows this to happen. Currently the Supreme Court requires contested fathers to take specific actions to have their "natural" rights recognized and if the State permissibly denies this opportunity then the natural father is left without rights. The opinion that provides for this essentially denies the reality of natural rights and makes the legal rights in the legal marriage superior to natural rights.

The logic used to do this is nothing more than a perversion of legal logic designed to support the ideology of State's rights. It is a victory for Statists who believe that all power is vested in the States. In reality, this opinion grants the States authority to deny the natural rights of American citizens and that should NEVER EVER happen. Natural rights should always be acknowledged and only denied where appropriately allowed.

## Chapter 6 — THE NATURAL RIGHTS CLAUSE

What is most important here is that the natural rights of parents comes before the legal rights of parents. There is of course an inherent harm to the husband who was probably without the knowledge that he was not the natural father. We recognize the pain in this and do not have ready answers here. We only know that the current system placing the legal marriage over the natural rights of parents is NOT the correct answer.

Where a person adopts a child, that person should, upon completing the process, be a fully vested parent protected by this amendment. No adoption should ever be allowed over the objection of a fit parent who is willing to take on full responsibility for the child.

Relatives of the child, when they have shown a willingness and ability over time to meet the child's minimum basic needs, and have established a parent-child bond, should receive parental rights protections when they are doing so in the absence of a fit parent.

This should never happen where there is an agreement between that relative and a natural or fully vested legal parent to temporarily care for the child. Just because a non-parent establishes a bond with a child as strong as that between parents and child does not mean that the bond is protected over that of the natural or legal parents.

# Chapter 7

## THE CARE CUSTODY CONTROL AND POSSESSION CLAUSE

*4. Minor children have the right to be in the care, custody, control, and possession of their fit parents equally, and where no fit parents exist, to be in the care, custody, control, and possession of the State. All other rights with which the minor child is endowed but is incapable of exercising are to be held in trust by fit parents in the first instance and by the State only where no fit parent exists.*

There is a lot of confusion about what "rights" children have. Many people want to create a large emotionally charged list of items such as children have a right to stability (status quo) or they have a right to choose their parents in divorce. These feel good concepts are NOT constitutional rights. These are also not rights that are for the state to give to the child.

Children do have constitutional rights. What they don't have is the ability to intelligently exercise most of these rights.

Everybody has the constitutional right to contract with other people. Most of us contract our labor in exchange for money. Children are prohibited from entering most contracts precisely because they do not have the mental capacity to protect themselves in a contractual relationship.

It is recognized that a contract between an adult and a minor child is such an unequal agreement that it can't be legally valid.

## Protecting Parent-Child Bonds

The parents of that child have the right to sign contracts on their child's behalf because parents have the responsibility to care for their children until they are able to do so for themselves. Therefore, minor children don't have a right to contract; they have a right to have a parent contract on their behalf. Children's rights are mostly of this nature.

Adults can under some circumstances be placed under the custody of the state where their right to be free from constraint is restricted. There is a large body of law and established constitutional opinion in this area. Except for these limited exceptions adults have a constitutional right to be free from constraint. Minor children, on the other hand, do not have the right to be free from constraint.

The rights that minor children do have are to be in the care, custody, and control of a parent or of the state as last resort. If we allowed minor children to be free from constraint there are countless ways that they would end up hurting themselves simply because they don't know any better. Modern science has proven that their brains do not have the physical structure necessary to know better. Unless states chose to lower the age of majority, children have no business deciding where or with whom they live.

What is even more surprising, but somehow, at the same time, unsurprising is that the brains of teenagers go through massive physical changes lasting into their early twenties and these changes limit their ability to accurately judge the consequences of their actions. In many situations teenagers are less equipped to make decisions than pre-teens.

Many people will tell you these things as folk wisdom. We have all witnessed teenage behaviors that defy all logic and support these claims. And, we have long had laws that restrict what minors can and cannot do based on this folk wisdom. What we have today is sound science that proves this folk wisdom and what's more, the science links this wisdom to actual physical changes in the brain that can be imaged and mapped.

With teens, this is very troubling because it comes with a host

## Chapter 7 — THE CARE CUSTODY CONTROL AND POSSESSION CLAUSE

of hormonal changes that biologically drive them to behaviors with lifelong consequences such as pregnancy, acts of aggression, and excessive risk taking.

For these reasons, it is vitally important that parents retain full authority to parent their children at least until the age of 18 even though the science might indicate a need into the early twenties. Parents absolutely need their full parental authority to have the greatest opportunity to protect their teens from poor decision-making during this crucial time.

This is especially true in the face of Divorce Courts that like to have teenage children choose between their parents. They take children who are at their most vulnerable and ask them to make decisions that will have lifelong impacts without any concern over the real harm that is being done to these children. The court is in essence saying that, even though we know you are incapable of entering into a contract on your own behalf because you don't have the capacity to weigh all the variables, in this instance where the stakes are so much higher, the variables so much greater, and the outside influences on your thinking so much greater we think you should go ahead and make the decision yourself, it's easier for the court that way.

Our children need our parental protection and the only way we can provide this protection is if our rights as parents are protected. This is even more important with teenagers again because they are going through changes that make them simultaneously more independent and more vulnerable. They are learning how to be independent adults but that very independence places them at greater risk and simultaneously reduces a parent's ability to protect them. Young children have a literal and physical dependency on adults that teenagers don't have. This dependence that young children have provides parents with much greater ability to protect them from harm.

Once the literal and physical dependency begins to diminish in the teen years, parents are left with emotional and financial dependencies as the primary means to enforce their authority in an effort to protect their children. This period is an eye blink in the

## Protecting Parent-Child Bonds

life of a child and of a parent. Too many courts intervene during this time with their long drawn out process. They limit parents' ability to protect their children and they ask children to make decisions that can haunt them for the rest of their lives. For this reason, it is crucial that we minimize the ability of courts to intervene during these crucial periods. We must NOT rob fit parents of the ability to protect their children, not for a day, nor an hour, nor even a minute. That is all it takes sometimes to rob a child of their protection and for a child to forever alter their lives.

The United States Supreme Court has said as recently as 2000 that it is beyond a doubt that parents have a constitutional right to the care, custody, and control of their minor children. Most reasonable people would argue that possession time with their child is to be found either in the term "custody", in the term "control", or in both terms.

Divorce Courts routinely treat possession as something altogether different. Divorce Courts routinely grant both parents "custody" but then limit one parent's possession time. More often than you would think, this possession time is dramatically limited or even prohibited altogether to fit parents based on nothing more than a judge's whim. Too often parents go into custody battles and win "joint-custody" only to find that the term "joint custody" has almost no meaning in divorce courts. It is nothing more than a feel good phrase that lets parents feel like they won something as they are losing most and sometimes all of their rights when they have done nothing wrong.

For these reasons, we have expanded on the Supreme Court phrase "care, custody, and control" with the term "possession" so that everybody will be absolutely clear that fit parent have equal right to possession of their children.

It is clear that when children become adults they will have all the rights of adults in America. We have made clear in this clause that all children have those rights from birth and that it is each parents' job to hold these rights in trust. This job belongs to nobody else except the fit parents and the State only in the absence of fit parents. While a parent may ask "the village" to help, final

## Chapter 7 — THE CARE CUSTODY CONTROL AND POSSESSION CLAUSE

accountablility and authority rests with the parents not "the villiage."

It is the parents' role to make sure that these rights when exercised are exercised in the best interest of the minor child. That means that in the normal course of events nobody is to challenge a parent's right to do so. And nobody is to question the parent's determination of best interest of the minor child. Only upon probable cause to believe that a parent is acting outside of the child's interests may the State temporarily intervene and even then the State MUST prove the parent is acting outside of the basic requirements and minimum standards required for a child's best interest before taking any permanent or long-term action.

Parents are without doubt the primary caretakers and caregivers for their minor children and the State generally has NO authority to intervene in these activities. It is each parents' natural right and they are each generally endowed by their creator or by nature with a drive and determination to care for their children. And, while the sexes may exercise this drive and determination in differing ways, each way is valid, and the differences must be afforded equal protection under the law.

# Chapter 8

## THE HEALTH SAFETY AND WELFARE CLAUSE

> *5. Nothing in this Amendment shall be construed as limiting the State from setting minimum, equally applicable, standards or regulation concerning the general health, safety, and welfare of its citizens. When rights between parents are in conflict and the State is asked to intervene, that intervention shall be the least detrimental to these rights. Where a valid question of harm to the child exists, the State may act to protect the child for the briefest time necessary to protect the child from that immediate harm.*

The Health, Safety, and Welfare Clause is designed to ensure that the proper and legitimate government authority necessary to protect the general health and welfare of its citizens is not prohibited. Let us not lose sight as to why this is so. In order for people to be able to exercise their rights, laws are required to ensure this ability. Therefore, as with all amendments and protected rights, there is room for restriction of these rights for this purpose. In the case of fundamental constitutional rights, which parental rights are, the State may only act to restrict those rights in very tightly managed ways. For instance, even though parents determine how their children are to be educated, the State has a role in setting minimum educational standards that apply equally to all parents and children.

The right to contract for labor is a strongly protected fundamental right that is routinely curtailed for health and safety issues that apply to all worksites of similar circumstances. Nobody can legally contract to work in a mine, for instance, where the contract exempts state or federal health and safety laws. Any contract of that type would be legally unenforceable. The right of people to contract with others is permissibly limited under these very narrowly tailored and limited situations.

Additionally, this clause ensures that disputes between fit parents, when addressed by the State, must be handled in a manner that meets the strictest standards of constitutional review. This is to ensure that parental rights receive the utmost protection and that States never again use the excuse that two parents don't agree to deny either of those parents' rights.

And finally, the last statement in this amendment makes clear that when there is real probable cause to believe that a child is in clear and present danger, the State is empowered under its normal police powers to step in to prevent that harm and to protect that child from harm by taking the child into protective custody. Generally, this should only be done under a warrant showing probable cause. However, there are well-established principles and respected rulings that allow for immediate action by the State if the danger is of an immediate nature. (The term harm should always be interpreted as "clear and present danger" in the context of this Amendment.)

This last statement is intended to make clear that this state intervention is allowed on a temporary basis only. The State is allowed the briefest time to conduct an investigation upon probable cause and to place the child into protective custody during that brief period.

Extensions to this brief period of time may only be established by Court order upon continuing probable cause and the briefest period of time necessary to bring credible charges against a parent. Parents are to be afforded an opportunity to be heard in this matter at the soonest possible time after the child is taken into custody if the child is to remain separated from the parent. Following a speedy trial, with proper constitutional protections, where the parent is not found guilty, that parent's rights must be restored and that parent not further prejudiced.

## Chapter 8 — THE HEALTH SAFETY AND WELFARE CLAUSE

Parental rights exist under the well-understood and accepted policy that people are innocent until proven guilty. Parental rights are established and respected until that parent is found unfit. The same level of due process required to keep someone jailed pending trial should be required before the State may keep a child away from a fit parent.

The privacy rights of parents and children, the sanctity of the parent-child bond, the free association rights of parents and children are too sacred to be disposed of based on fear that something bad might happen. Too many children are being harmed by this fear today through out-of-control child protective agencies, divorce courts, and reactive state legislation.

While it is always terrible when children are harmed, we must recognize that more children are harmed when in the hands of unfeeling, uncaring, sterile government agencies or divorce court process than are harmed by fit parents. And, we must recognize that there is some harm that is beyond the government's reach to do anything about. There is inherent harm in divorce and the process of going through divorce but the government should not be participating in trying to control the parties to prevent this harm.

There is harm in moving children multiple times, yet the government cannot reach into a married family to prevent this; they should not be allowed to reach into private family decisions that create perceived harm because it does not meet the ideal nuclear "Leave it to Beaver" family structure. Depending on your preference, either God or Nature created incredibly strong parent-child bonds that establish a natural tendency for parents to provide the protection, care and nurturing that children need. While this nature is not absolute, it is the best hope for our children and should never be replaced with sterile government process except as the very last resort.

# Chapter 9

## THE AUTHORS' FINAL WORDS

*No power has ever been found to be more suited to the protection of children than the natural bonding of parent and child. No State agency or divorce court judge can ever hope to match the level of care and devotion created by that parent-child bond. Supporting this Amendment is your opportunity to ensure that the parent-child bonds that play such a strong role in the lives of our children are protected to the utmost of our ability as a nation.*

*This book and this Amendment provides you an opportunity to tell your government that the interests of children must be protected and that those interests are best protected by fit parents with guaranteed parental rights.*

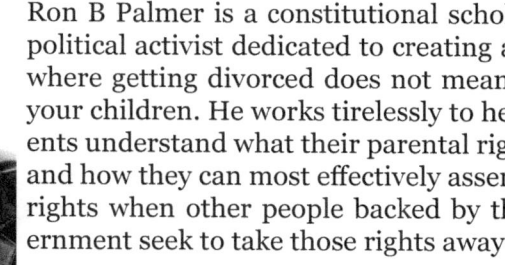

Ron B Palmer is a constitutional scholar and political activist dedicated to creating a world where getting divorced does not mean losing your children. He works tirelessly to help parents understand what their parental rights are and how they can most effectively assert those rights when other people backed by the government seek to take those rights away.

In his last book with co-author and wife Sherry L Palmer, Ron laid out the constitutional history of parental rights and clarified the source of parental rights based on 90 cited U.S. Supreme Court opinions and other Federal Appellate and State Supreme Court opinions. He provided sound arguments that empower parents being deprived of their rights to argue their rights effectively at all levels of our State and Federal Courts.

As promised in that book, this book leads the charge for greater recognition of the rights parents have today and for strengthening those rights based on the many ways that States have sought to inappropriately deprive parents of their children. This book is the beginning of a political statement that parents' rights to their children are Natural Fundamental rights that must be given the utmost of respect by all branches of state and federal governments.

This book also sets out the rights that children have to free and equal association with both fit parents that should not be invaded by the State or infringed upon by another parent.

When this Amendment is passed parents will not have to reference countless Supreme Court opinions, they will only have to say I have 28th Amendment rights to be a parent and no Divorce Court can ever deprive me of those rights so long as I am a fit parent.

This book is intended to be a tool for citizen activists who want change to the sytem but who may struggle with all of the technical arguments. Now all you have to do to support change is hand this book to your politician of choice and say, "I want this, make it happen."

 Sherry L Palmer is the mother of four children and one stepchild. She holds a Bachelor's Degree in Public Policy and Community Service from the University of North Texas. She successfully owned and ran a medical transcription service and retail outlets. Since her experience in the family courts she has become a trusted advisor, coach, and consultant to attorneys, parents, legislators, and other professionals.

Her expertise in this area comes from years of custody battles where she had to act *pro se* the majority of the time. She experienced extremes of judicial, agency, and attorney misconduct. She endured extremes of procedural delays and procedural mistreatment of *pro se* litigants. After becoming aware of parental alienation and parental rights she became more effective and was able to turn her case around and to restore her time with her children and stop the mental torture, financial bleeding, and disruptions in her family.

She knew in her heart that what was being done in the courts and how it was being done was fundamentally wrong, while not having the bandwidth to prove it as she was going through the battles, she vowed she would take the time to change things for future generations. Since then she has spent the time painstakingly documenting why these practices are both morally and constitutionally wrong, and shares this with others all throughout the U.S. and internationally.

She has combined her strengths in research and activism/advocacy with her husband to make a strong team that creates constitutional and moral arguments for change. She knows that once enough people become aware fewer people will fall victim, the activism follows...and one day Parental Rights will be as widely accepted as Miranda Rights are today. Sherry intends to make sure that others are not left with the same system that she and her children were forced to suffer through...but rather one that protects the interests of both the children and parents and operates within the boundaries of the Constitution.

## NOT In the Child's Best Interest

This is another amazing book by Ron and Sherry Palmer designed to help those fighting for child custody under the current system. The United States Supreme Court has said some really great things about parental rights and you can use what they have said to help you retain or regain your parental rights even in divorce.

If you really want to understand the current state of constitutional rights for parents then this book is for you. In an easy to read format, it takes you through some of the history of child custody issues. It shows how child custody went from being a property interest to being a liberty interest. It shows how the Courts thinking about child custody and parental rights has evolved and how divorce court thinking has failed to keep up.

Ron and Sherry take a complicated issue and transform it into something easily understandable by parents. Even still, the book is crammed full of US Supreme Court citations that your attorney can leverage immediately to help you in your custody battles today.

Politicians who attempt to improve the family law system in this country will inevitably be slammed with special interest groups from all sides, each trying to preserve or gain an advantage for their interest group. Ron and Sherry have only one interest group, the group of fit parents. Ron and Sherry have only one agenda, to ensure that fit parents have equal rights to raise their children free from unwarranted government intrusion into their lives. This book is a tremendous resource for countering the special interest groups and preparing constitutionally sound responses to their arguments.

Everyone touched by the family law system, whether parent, attorney, judge, or politician, will benefit from the extensive and down-to-earth constitutional analysis this book provides. Available on Amazon.com.

## Fix Family Courts Services

Not only are Ron and Sherry avid writers and speakers they are also skilled divorce and custody coaches who provide a range of specialized services for those in need, such as:

- **Initial Consultation:** One hour of one-on-one time with your divorce coach. This time will be used to determine where you are in the process and to provide you with some options for changing your outcomes.

- **Strategy Map:** What is the strategy map and how does it help me?

    The strategy map helps you understand the full process and pinpoints where you are in that process. Only when this is understood can you make good strategic choices about what to do next.

    Every parent has different goals based on their own family situations pre and post-divorce. Clarifying these goals makes them achievable and identifies your next steps.

    Unlike your attorney, we do NOT make decisions for you. What your divorce coach does is to make sure that you know how the system works, what your options are at each stage of the process, what the risks are for each option, and how best to communicate these to your attorney.

    Your personalized strategy map developed by your divorce coach keeps you from making life altering decisions for you and your child in the dark.

- **Direct Coaching:** You will have one-on-one time with your divorce coach who will help clear away the legal murk and make your choices more clear.

    You will get plain language explanations of how the system works and why certain things are happening to you at this very moment.

You will get direct help in implementing your strategy at every step of the way when and as you need it.

You will learn of strategies that go beyond what the legal system or your attorney can offer.

- **Training Motions:** Ron & Sherry have produced training motions that are written just as your attorney might write them making the specific arguments necessary to promote your fundamental rights in your custody case. These motions have been used by attorneys across the country with only minor modifications to convert them into legal documents in local jurisdictions.

    Hard hitting motions put judges on the spot and require them to answer or be overturned on appeal

    Real constitutional questions leveraging local laws that require judges to answer

    Even if your judge is the worst and will never do the right thing, these motions set your judge up to be overturned on appeal

    These motions put power into your hands with little extra work on your attorney's part

    As always, we provide one-on-one coaching to your attorney to prepare them to use this power for you

- **Written Arguments:** Attorneys are so busy working the legal system that they have very little time or energy to develop new approaches and new constitutional arguments.

    Creating new approaches and new constitutional arguments is our primary focus

    We can provide these arguments in writing where your attorney can simply cut and paste into your legal pleadings

    From crafting short arguments on specific targets to crafting entire pleadings, motions, appeal documents, etc. we help your attorney bring the power of these arguments to bear for you in your specific case. (Available only if you have an attorney)

- **Attorney Support:** It's not enough to simply craft new approaches and arguments, your attorney must feel comfortable with making these arguments during trial.

    We work one-on-one with your attorney to help them articulate your strategic arguments

    We provide your attorney with the case citations necessary to give these arguments real legal teeth

    We ghost write your documents. We craft the constitutional arguments to your needs in the legal documents appropriate to the specific stage of your case. Your attorney reviews, modifies as appropriate, and submits them under his/her authority

    We advise and assist your attorney in crafting a comprehensive strategy using constitutional arguments and novel in family law but well-established legal tools to give you the advantage in your case

    We serve as an extenstion of your attorney's legal team providing specific constitutional expertise behind the scenes and even at trial

    We can attend your hearings, sit at the table with your attorney, and provide real time strategic guidance and constitutional support during the moments when it really counts for you

    We can re-frame your case, craft questions for your attorney to ask witnesses and teach you how to testify with confidence and effectiveness

Please remember, WE ARE NOT ATTORNEYS, we can NOT give legal advice. However, we can provide research, logical argument, and case citations to your attorney reducing the time they spend on your case and increasing their ability to effectively argue in support of your parental rights as guaranteed under our Constitution.

We can act as a part of your attorney's legal team under their legal supervision to craft your strategy and legal documents. We can even attend your hearings and assist your attorney as they have to respond in real time.

Your divorce attorney is unlikely to be a constitutional expert on child-custody issues. We are the experts and have demonstrated our expertise in writing, in the courtroom, and in successfully helping parents keep and regain custody of their children.

Please, don't ever assume or trust that any attorney is protecting your constitutional rights until you have verified their beliefs and actions.

# The National Family Law Policy Center

nflpc.org

Ron and Sherry have founded The National Family Law Policy Center as a non-profit to promote a national policy of protection for parental rights and parent-child bonds. This center is designed to be a source of information for legislators, judges, attorneys, and parents for promoting and expanding on sound constitutional family law policy.

This is where a national policy on parental rights will be crafted and promoted. While family law is a state issue, the US Constitution sets clear limits on what states may and may not do. The Policy Center will establish and promote a baseline family law policy that will bring uniform recognition of the boundaries beyond which no state may go. It will promote uniformity in state family law codes that will allow parents to move freely between states without fear of losing rights simply by moving to another state.

The Policy Center is designed to help businesses protect their employees from the ravages of arbitrary and corrupt family law systems. It is designed to help our economy and our country by removing a major detriment to attention and productivity. The policies it promotes will help remove a major source of workplace accidents that cause economic and environmental damage often with significant loss of life.

The devistation wrought by family law courts is not limited to our families, it is felt by businesses and by everyone in our economy who pay for the loss of productivity and the accidents which directly result from the unnatural stress created when a parent's children are stolen from them by their own government.

You can help end this devastation by making a donation to this effort or even by becoming a member and supporting these activities through your active membership.

Bring the Policy Center to the attention of your employer and ask your employer to include them in your company's giving campaign. Ask your employer to give directly or to contact The Policy Center directly to find out more about how The Policy Center works to protect businesses and the economy as well as parents and their children.

Get more information at www.nflpc.org.

Thank You for your kind and generous support of these efforts.

www.ingramcontent.com/pod-product-compliance
Lightning Source LLC
Chambersburg PA
CBHW071758170526
45167CB00003B/1087